GIA━━━━━━━━OLD TESTAMENT

LESSONS ON LIVING FROM
ABRAHAM

A devotional by
WOODROW KROLL

BACK TO THE BIBLE
Publishing

ABRAHAM
published by Back to the Bible
©1998 by Woodrow Kroll

International Standard Book Number
0-8474-0685-7

Edited by Rachel Derowitsch
Cover concept by Robert Greuter
& Associates

Unless otherwise noted, all Scripture is
taken from the New King James Version.
Copyright © 1979, 1980, 1982,
Thomas Nelson, Inc.
Used by permission.

ALL RIGHTS RESERVED
No part of this publication may be repro-
duced, stored in a retrieval system or
transmitted, in any form or by any
means—electronic, mechanical photo-
copying, recording or otherwise—except
for brief quotations in printed reviews or
articles, without the prior written permission of the publisher.

For information:
BACK TO THE BIBLE
POST OFFICE BOX 82808
LINCOLN, NEBRASKA 68501

2 3 4 5 6 7 8 9—04 03 02 01 00 99 98

Printed in the USA

CONTENTS

DAY 1

Genesis 11:31

And Terah took his son Abram and his grand-son Lot, the son of Haran, and his daughter-in-law Sarai, his son Abram's wife, and they went out with them from Ur of the Chaldeans to go to the land of Canaan; and they came to Haran and dwelt there.

The First Step

The Chinese philosopher Lao-Tse once said, "A journey of a thousand miles must begin with a single step." While we all tend to focus on the destination, the time it will take to complete our journey or the items we need to accomplish it, the trip itself cannot begin until we're willing to take the first step.

Abraham was willing to take that first step. True, Haran was not his ultimate destination. Some have faulted him for stopping short of Canaan. We don't know for sure why he didn't go on. Perhaps his father, Terah, was not physically able to continue. We do know that Terah died in Haran. It is also possible that Abraham got temporarily sidetracked. Circumstances may have caused him momentarily to forget that God's call was to Canaan, not Haran. But we should never forget that at least Abraham took the first step toward his ultimate destination.

You, too, may have a goal in mind. Perhaps God has burdened your heart to teach a Sunday school class, to receive more training in the Bible or to witness to your neighbor. But as you look at that objective, you don't see how you can reach it. The way seems too long or the process too difficult. The answer is to take the first step. Even though the way may not seem clear at the moment, you can be sure that if you don't begin, you'll never finish.

Trust God to provide whatever is needed along the way. As you step out in faith, expect God to step in with power. As you take the first step, He will make sure all the other steps fall in place.

The hardest step is always the first step.

Reflections/Prayer Requests

_____

_____

_____

_____

_____

_____

_____

_____

DAY 2

Genesis 12:1-3

Now the LORD had said to Abram: "Get out of your country, from your kindred and from your father's house, to a land that I will show you. I will make you a great nation; I will bless you and make your name great; and you shall be a blessing. I will bless those who bless you, and I will curse him who curses you; and in you all the families of the earth shall be blessed."

The Greatest Calling

An oil company needed a suave public relations man for its office in Asia. After interviewing several candidates, the officials decided to ask a local missionary to take the position. Company executives met with this man of unusual gifts. Whatever they proposed, however, his answer was always "no." "What's wrong?" asked one interviewer. "Isn't the salary big enough?" The missionary replied, "The salary is big enough, but the job isn't."

Abraham was faced with a similar option. He could have stayed in Haran and become a leading citizen. As a natural-born leader, he may have become ruler of the city. Most certainly, as a clever businessman, he would have become wealthy and lived in luxury and ease. But all that was insignificant compared to what God had in mind for him. By obeying God's call, he became a blessing to the whole world.

God still calls people today. Maybe He is calling you to be a pastor or missionary or church leader. On the other hand, He may be calling you to be an active witness for Him in your place of secular employment. But you also may be facing alternatives. Another position may offer a bigger salary, a bigger office or less hassle. Don't be fooled. Seek God's direction. Wherever He is calling you will bring the greatest blessing—to you and to those around you.

When God calls, accepting anything else is no bargain.

Reflections/Prayer Requests

DAY 3

Genesis 12:5

Then Abram took Sarai his wife and Lot his brother's son, and all their possessions that they had gathered, and the people whom they had acquired in Haran, and they departed to go to the land of Canaan. So they came to the land of Canaan.

Obey All the Way

Louis Cassels once wrote, "Obey . . . take up your cross . . . deny yourself . . . it all sounds very hard. It is hard. Anyone who tells you differently is peddling spiritual soothing syrup, not real Christianity." Perhaps that's why so many Christians stop short of complete obedience.

Even Abraham struggled with this problem. As a great man of faith, Abraham had obeyed when God told him to "get out of your country" (Gen. 12:1). Immediately he packed up his possessions and left. But God also had said, "from your *kindred* and from your *father's house*, to a land that I will show you" (emphasis mine). It was here that Abraham stumbled. Genesis 12:5 notes that he took "Lot his brother's son" with him. Perhaps Abraham felt responsible for his nephew since Haran, Lot's father, had died. But this act of incomplete obedience became a cause of grief for himself (Gen. 13:5-7) and eventually for his nephew as well. Lot lost everything but his two daughters in the destruction of Sodom (Gen. 19:12-26).

Obedience is often hard, but partial obedience will not make things easier. The lack of total obedience may seem justified—especially if it involves a family member. It may even seem as if we are shirking our duty to loved ones if we do as God has instructed us. But God has a reason for every command, and not to obey Him completely always means forfeiting a blessing.

What is God asking of you today? What obedience is He prompting from you right now? Are you willing to obey all the way? Remember, incomplete obedience is the half-brother of disobedience.

Trust and obey—there's no other way.

Reflections/Prayer Requests

_____

_____

_____

_____

_____

_____

_____

_____

DAY 4

Genesis 12:8

And he moved from there to the mountain east of Bethel, and he pitched his tent with Bethel on the west and Ai on the east; there he built an altar to the LORD and called on the name of the LORD.

Pledge Your Allegiance

Many professional athletes proudly wear the corporate logo or company colors of those who sponsor them. They have no qualms at all in identifying themselves with the products and purposes of those who finance their careers.

When Abraham pitched his tents near Bethel, he boldly identified himself with the Lord. God not only called him to leave family and all that was familiar, but also provided for his needs along the way. In response, Abraham built an altar to God. This was not only an act of worship but also a public declaration to everyone who saw it that he was a worshiper of Yahweh. Furthermore, he "called on the name of the LORD"—that is, he publicly acknowledged his commitment to and need for the God of Israel.

As Christians, we are to boldly identify ourselves with the Lord as well. Be prepared. This may cost you the friendship of those who prefer the praises of the world. It may mean that you will experience ridicule and rejection. But Jesus reminds us, "Whoever confesses Me before men, him the Son of Man also will confess before the angels of God. But he who denies Me before men will be denied before the angels of God" (Luke 12:8-9).

Make your allegiance known. Wherever you may be, with whomever you may be, refuse to hide your commitment to the One who loves you and provides for your salvation. Jesus suffered the shame of the cross for you; be willing to suffer the ridicule of the world for Him.

There's no place in God's service for secret agents.

Reflections/Prayer Requests

_____

_____

_____

_____

_____

_____

_____

_____

_____

DAY 5

Genesis 12:12-13

"Therefore it will happen, when the Egyptians see you, that they will say, 'This is his wife'; and they will kill me, but they will let you live. Please say you are my sister, that it may be well with me for your sake, and that I may live because of you."

The Wrong Kind of Help

A little boy asked his mother, "What is a lie?" "A lie," she replied, "is an abomination to the Lord—but a very present help in time of trouble."

Abraham apparently agreed. Faced with a famine in the land of Canaan, he moved his household down to Egypt. Out of fear for his life, he told the Egyptians that Sarah was his sister and persuaded her to go along with his lie. When Pharaoh heard of her beauty, and thinking her unmarried, he took her into his harem. Abraham was on the brink of saving his life but losing his wife. Fortunately God intervened and Pharaoh learned the truth in time. Abraham, however, was rebuked and forced to leave the land. In the end, his lie earned him nothing but contempt and disgrace.

Often we are tempted to lie our way out of a tight spot. Perhaps at work a "small lie" will help us avoid admitting we made a mistake. Or at home "bending the truth" may seemingly help us avoid a scene. But resorting to subterfuge always ends up causing us more heartache than help.

When tempted to lie, remember that what seems like a "very present help" will ultimately be "an abomination to the Lord." Lies always result in more hurt and hassle in the long run. That kind of help you can do without. Instead, tell the truth and trust God. He'll take care of you.

A lie appears to offer help, but in reality only delivers harm.

Reflections/Prayer Requests

_____

_____

_____

_____

_____

_____

_____

_____

_____

_____

_____

DAY 6

Genesis 13:1-2

*Then Abram went up from Egypt, he and his
wife and all that he had, and Lot with him, to
the South. Abram was very rich in livestock,
in silver, and in gold.*

Blessed Promises

William Penn, the founder of the com-
monwealth of Pennsylvania, was well
liked by the Indians. Once they told him he
could have as much of their land as he
could encompass on foot in a single day.
So early the next morning, he started out
and walked until late that night. When he
finally went to claim his land, the Indians
were greatly surprised, for they didn't
think he would take them seriously. But
they kept their promise and gave him a
large tract of land. Today that area is
Philadelphia.

God also made a promise to Abraham:
"I will bless you" (Gen. 12:2-3). Even
though Abraham made mistakes and
sometimes failed to trust the Lord fully,
God never went back on His promise. He
blessed Abraham materially until he was
"very rich in livestock, in silver, and in
gold." More important, He blessed Abraham spiritually. God declared in Genesis
22:17-18, "In blessing I will bless you, and
in multiplying I will multiply your descendants as the stars of the heaven and as the

14

sand which is on the seashore; and your descendants shall possess the gate of their enemies. In your seed all the nations of the earth shall be blessed, because you have obeyed My voice." Through Abraham's descendants came the Messiah, who brought the blessing of salvation to all nations.

God continues to bless today just as He has promised. Though we quickly forget them, God's blessings are all around us. He allows some of us to be the stewards of His material blessings, but He gives all of us the opportunity to enjoy His spiritual blessings. His salvation, forgiveness and lovingkindness are promised blessings that God will never forget.

Rejoice today in your blessings. Rest confidently in the truth that what God has promised, He will never take away.

Enjoy the riches that are yours because you are His.

Reflections/Prayer Requests

_____

_____

_____

_____

_____

DAY 7

Genesis 13:5-7

Lot also, who went with Abram, had flocks and herds and tents. Now the land was not able to support them, that they might dwell together, for their possessions were so great. . . . And there was strife between the herdsmen of Abram's livestock and the herdsmen of Lot's livestock. The Canaanites and the Perizzites then dwelt in the land.

Someone Is Watching

Whether we know it or not, people are watching us. One day as a woman was crossing the street at London Station, an old man stopped her. He said, "Excuse me, Ma'am, but I want to thank you." She looked surprised and asked, "Thank me?" He replied, "Yes'm. I used to be a ticket collector, and whenever you went by you always gave me a cheerful smile and a good morning. I knew that smile must come from inside somewhere. Then one morning I saw a little Bible in your hand. So I bought one, too, and I found Jesus."

Abraham was also very conscious that he was being watched. Problems had developed between his nephew, Lot, and himself. They came to possess so many sheep and cattle between them that the land was not able to support them all. It reached the point where the herdsmen of

Abraham and the herdsmen of Lot began to quarrel over the best grazing lands. All the while, the Canaanites and the Perizzites, who lived in the land as well, were watching. Abraham knew that he represented Yahweh, the Lord God of heaven, before these pagan families. As a result, he immediately sought a way to bring peace to the situation.

Neither your church family nor your personal family are immune from problems. But how you choose to deal with those problems can encourage or hinder others who are watching. Your actions can even influence their eternal destiny. Always choose the way of peace. Let the God of peace rule not only in your heart but in all your relationships.

A family at peace is the best witness to the Lord of Peace.

Reflections/Prayer Requests

_____

_____

_____

_____

_____

_____

_____

DAY 8

Genesis 13:8-9

So Abram said to Lot, "Please let there be no strife between you and me, and between my herdsmen and your herdsmen; for we are brethren. Is not the whole land before you? Please separate from me. If you take the left, then I will go to the right; or, if you go to the right, then I will go to the left."

I've Got Rights

Everyone seems concerned about their rights. Whatever the issue, someone is sure to claim that he or she has the right to engage in it. Someone else will maintain that if this person asserts his rights, it will violate *their* rights. It's no wonder that one social commentator observed, "The search for the good has yielded to the search for rights."

When it came time to separate from his nephew, Abraham certainly could have demanded his rights. As the patriarch in the family, Abraham had the right of first choice about where he wanted to go, but he graciously allowed his younger relative to choose instead. When Lot selfishly chose the lush, fertile valleys, Abraham could have legitimately protested that this flagrant unfairness was a violation of his rights. Instead, he simply packed up his belongings and moved to the more barren

18

hill country. Obviously, Abraham was more interested in preserving his relationship with Lot than he was in exercising his rights.

God does not assure His children that we will always have our rights recognized. The apostle Paul urges us, "Let nothing be done through selfish ambition or conceit, but in lowliness of mind let each esteem others better than himself" (Phil. 2:3). In other words, let the rights of others be first in your mind, and God will take care of the rest.

If your "rights" have been trampled upon, turn them over to the Lord. A loving relationship with the important people in your life will ultimately be more satisfying than protecting your rights.

Be more concerned about doing right than having rights.

Reflections/Prayer Requests

_____

_____

_____

_____

_____

_____

_____

DAY 9

Genesis 13:14-15

And the L$_{ORD}$ said to Abram, after Lot had separated from him: "Lift your eyes now and look from the place where you are—northward, southward, eastward, and westward; for all the land which you see I give to you and your descendants forever."

A Place Called Home

In late summer the migration of the monarch butterfly occurs. If you're in the right place at the right time, you can see hundreds of them clinging to tree limbs and shrubbery as the flock journeys to a remote mountain site in central Mexico. Scientists have found 16 of these sites, ranging from one to ten acres each, within a 100-mile radius, where millions of butterflies from North America spend the winter. No one knows how butterflies find their way there. Each generation that migrates is new and has never been there before. Yet something programmed into their tiny bodies directs them to a place they have never seen, but is a home they instinctively know they must find.

The Jews have the same attitude toward their homeland of Israel, and it all began with Abraham. God gave him a plot of land—not just to this Jewish patriarch, but to his "descendants forever." Even though they are now spread throughout the world, Jews still long to return to this small oasis. For some, it's just for a visit; for others, it's to start life over again. But for Jews, wherever they may live, Israel is home.

That same instinct for home should burn in the hearts of Christians. For us, home is not a country on earth; it's a destination called heaven. While Abraham and his descendants were promised a land, all who receive Jesus Christ as Savior are promised an eternal dwelling place (John 14:2).

Take comfort in the thought that you have a home in heaven. Each day brings you closer to home—not to visit but to live. God has reserved a dwelling place that will fulfill the deepest longing of your heart. Rejoice!

Heaven is more than a city; it's a home.

Reflections/Prayer Requests

_____

_____

_____

_____

_____

_____

_____

DAY 10

Genesis 14:14

Now when Abram heard that his brother was taken captive, he armed his three hundred and eighteen trained servants who were born in his own house, and went in pursuit as far as Dan.

The Lord's Army

We live in violent times. The American Bar Association claims that crimes involving guns, drugs and juveniles are putting an unprecedented crunch on the nation's courts. Every 22 seconds someone in the United States is beaten, stabbed, shot, robbed, raped or killed. Nearly two million people every year become violent-crime victims.

Lot lived in violent times as well. Fortunately, he had an uncle with his own private army. When Abraham learned that the cities of Sodom and Gomorrah had been conquered and all their people taken captive, including his nephew, Lot, he armed his private militia. In a brilliant piece of military strategy, he overtook the enemy forces and surprised them at night. When morning arrived, the adversary was on the run and all were rescued, including Lot.

Most of us do not have relatives who can muster a private army. But Christians have something even better—we have the Lord. The psalmist says, "The angel of the LORD encamps all around those who fear Him, and delivers them" (Ps. 34:7). And again God's Word reminds us, "For He shall give His angels charge over you, to keep you in all your ways" (Ps. 91:11). Every believer dwells in the midst of God's protective care as represented by His angels.

When you find yourself beginning to be afraid, remind yourself that God's army is with you. God's angels stand guard over you. No enemy can ever truly harm you. The mighty army of the Lord has your safety as its responsibility. Don't be afraid. Remember Psalm 56:3: "Whenever I am afraid, I will trust in You."

Our safety rests not in the ability of man but in the army of God.

Reflections/Prayer Requests

_____

_____

_____

_____

_____

_____

DAY 11

Genesis 14:22-23

But Abram said to the king of Sodom, "I have lifted my hand to the LORD, God Most High, the Possessor of heaven and earth, that I will take nothing, from a thread to a sandal strap, and that I will not take anything that is yours, lest you should say, 'I have made Abram rich.'"

Making It God's Way

People often want to get rich quickly. In 1989 John Bennett established the Foundation for New Era Philanthropy. Under the guise of a non-profit foundation, he offered donors the opportunity to double their money within six to nine months. In 1994 he allowed nonprofit organizations to participate. This too-good-to-be-true offer brought waves of money from various institutions as well as philanthropists to support what turned out to be a pyramid scheme. In September 1997, Bennett was sentenced to prison for defrauding charities and others of $354 million.

Abraham also had the opportunity to gain more wealth quickly. Bera, king of Sodom, offered Abraham all the "loot" of the city in exchange for the people. But Abraham considered the source and declined. The opportunity to become even more wealthy was not worth the price of being indebted to the king of Sodom. His city was so wicked that it would shortly be destroyed by brimstone and fire. Abraham preferred to let God provide for his needs; he didn't need Sodom's money.

The desire to get rich can bring many pains and heartaches. The apostle Paul wrote to Timothy, "For the love of money is a root of all kinds of evil, for which some have strayed from the faith in their greediness, and pierced themselves through with many sorrows" (1 Tim. 6:10). The appetite for more and more can lead you into associations with people who can cause you irreparable spiritual harm.

If you find yourself in any relationship, business or personal, that is damaging your spiritual life, drop it immediately. It may mean taking a financial loss, but when you make your relationship with the Lord your most important priority, He will take care of all your other needs (Matt. 6:33).

God's wealth can't be found in Satan's treasury.

Reflections/Prayer Requests

_____

_____

_____

_____

_____

DAY 12

Genesis 15:1

After these things the word of the LORD came to Abram in a vision, saying, "Do not be afraid, Abram. I am your shield, your exceedingly great reward."

Fear Not

Fear is everywhere. Even people who appear brave, if they're honest, will admit to moments of immense fear.

During World War II, a military governor met with Gen. George Patton in Sicily. When he highly praised Patton for his courage and bravery, the general replied, "Sir, I am not a brave man—the truth is, I am a craven coward. I have never been within the sound of gunshot or in sight of battle in my whole life that I wasn't so scared that I had sweat in the palms of my hands." Patton's honesty is refreshing, but God offers the best solution for our fears.

Abraham was just as human as you and I. Even though he had 318 trained soldiers in his personal army and had just won a major victory over four mighty kings (Gen. 14:13-17), he still experienced times of apprehension and dread. That's why God said, "Do not be afraid." God then told Abraham why he need not be afraid: "I am your shield [to protect you from evil], your exceedingly great reward [to meet all your needs]."

Our fears fall into two broad categories. We fear that something will harm us or that we will suffer need in some way. God promises that He is sufficient for both of these concerns. The psalmist speaks of God's protection from evil when he says, "A thousand may fall at your side, and ten thousand at your right hand; but it shall not come near you" (Ps. 91:7). And in another psalm we are assured of God's provision: "The young lions lack and suffer hunger; but those who seek the LORD shall not lack any good thing" (34:10).

What troubles you today? Put aside your fears and trust God. The God of Abraham is sufficient both to protect you and to provide for all your needs.

Where God stands, fear falls.

Reflections/Prayer Requests

_____

_____

_____

_____

_____

_____

_____

_____

DAY 13

Genesis 15:2-4

But Abram said, "Lord GOD, what will You give me, seeing I go childless, and the heir of my house is Eliezer of Damascus?" Then Abram said, "Look, You have given me no offspring; indeed one born in my house is my heir!" And behold, the word of the LORD came to him, saying, "This one shall not be your heir, but one who will come from your own body shall be your heir."

I Wonder

Henry Drummond, a 19th-century Scottish evangelist, observed, "Christ never failed to distinguish between doubt and unbelief. Doubt is can't believe; unbelief is won't believe. Doubt is honesty; unbelief is obstinacy. Doubt is looking for light; unbelief is being content with darkness."

When God promised to bless him (Gen. 15:1), Abraham responded, "How are you going to do it?" This was not a lack of faith, because Abraham believed God was going to keep His promise; he simply didn't understand how God would do it. Since "blessings" were always believed to come through children (Ps. 127:3-5), and Abraham had none (nor from a human perspective did it look like he would have any), he inquired as to how God was going to do it. God honored that question and told him, "One who will come from your own body shall be your heir." Abraham was satisfied. The case was closed.

It's not wrong to ask questions about God's plan; it's only wrong to question the rightness of God's plan. There's a subtle but important difference here. It's only natural for people to want to know, "God, how do You plan to pull this off?" In essence Abraham said, "I'm to be the father of a great nation, and yet I have no children. I know You can do it, Lord. But I'd sure like to know how."

If you're wondering how God will work His will and His way in your life, it's perfectly legitimate to ask. But always ask in faith. Feel free to question how God is going to work out His plan, but never question His ability to work out that plan. The first is inquiring faith; the second is irreverent unbelief.

Doubt asks how; unbelief asks why.

Reflections/Prayer Requests

_____

_____

_____

_____

_____

_____

DAY 14

Genesis 15:13-14

Then He said to Abram: "Know certainly that your descendants will be strangers in a land that is not theirs, and will serve them, and they will afflict them four hundred years. And also the nation whom they serve I will judge; afterward they shall come out with great possessions."

We Win

Life can be tough; it can also be scary. Maybe you wonder where you'll ever find the courage to face a fearful future. That's the question someone asked Billy Graham; he responded, "I've read the last chapter of Revelation, and we win."

As God revealed to Abraham the fate of his descendants, it sounded less than exciting. For 400 years they would be the slaves of another nation. Have you ever wondered what kept them going when they were oppressed and mistreated by the Egyptians? Maybe it was God's promise, "I will judge; afterward they shall come out with great possessions." In other words, in the end, "you win."

Yes, along the way there would be hardships and affliction, but when Israel got to the bottom line, those who afflicted them would be judged and they would be rewarded. This was not a "maybe," but something God promised that Abraham could "know certainly."

Your life, too, is bound to have its share of heartache and sadness. No one can pass through their years on earth without some mistreatment and unfairness. You may even echo the cry of the prophet Habakkuk: "O LORD, how long shall I cry, and You will not hear? Even cry out to You, 'Violence!' And You will not save" (Hab. 1:2). In the midst of the pain, however, you must always cling to the unchangeable truth that in the end we win.

When you experience bone-crunching difficulties, meditate on verses such as 2 Corinthians 4:17-18 and Revelation 7:14-17 and 21:4. Take comfort in the truth that, despite what you may be going through right now, in the end, you win.

The present is bearable when we're confident that the future is glorious.

Reflections/Prayer Requests

_____

_____

_____

_____

_____

DAY 15

Genesis 15:15-16

Now as for you, you shall go to your fathers in peace; you shall be buried at a good old age. But in the fourth generation [your descendants] shall return here, for the iniquity of the Amorites is not yet complete.

The Patience of God

For the most part, people are very impatient. The moment the stoplight turns green, the driver behind us invariably honks his horn. You can just see the frustration and impatience in the faces of those caught in a long line at the grocery store checkout stand. Fortunately, God demonstrates a great deal more restraint than we do.

When God revealed to Abraham some things yet to come, He advised him that his descendants would not return to the land for four generations because "the iniquity of the Amorites" was not yet complete. Even though these people were pagans, God continued to demonstrate patience toward them. With Abraham dwelling in their midst (Gen. 13:7), there was always the possibility that individuals, if not the nation as a whole, might turn to the God of Abraham. While man might have brought swift judgment, God graciously gave these people over 400 more years to turn from their idolatry and embrace the living God.

The apostle Peter spoke of this same graciousness. He reminded his readers, "The Lord is not slack concerning His promise, as some count slackness, but is longsuffering toward us, not willing that any should perish but that all should come to repentance" (2 Pet. 3:9).

Satan loves to convince us that God's patience with us has come to an end. He tries to persuade us that we have sinned just one time too often and God has washed His hands of us. But we must reject this lie. While we must not abuse God's patience, He still stands ready to forgive and receive us back when we repent. Be confident that you can never deplete the patience of God, if your heart is pure and your repentance sincere.

The perverseness of man cannot exhaust the patience of God.

Reflections/Prayer Requests

_____

_____

_____

_____

_____

_____

DAY 16

Genesis 16:1-2

Now Sarai, Abram's wife, had borne him no children. And she had an Egyptian maidservant whose name was Hagar. So Sarai said to Abram, "See now, the LORD has restrained me from bearing children. Please, go in to my maid; perhaps I shall obtain children by her." And Abram heeded the voice of Sarai.

Running Ahead of God

A friend went to visit the great preacher Phillips Brooks and found him pacing the floor like a caged lion. His friend asked, "What's the trouble, Dr. Brooks?" He replied, "The trouble is that I'm in a hurry but God isn't."

Abraham could have identified with those feelings. God had promised him a son, but, from a human perspective, time was running out. In fact, with Abraham nearly 86 and Sarah 76 years old, most people would have said that time had already run out. Obviously God needed help. In the Ancient Near East, it was acceptable for a barren woman to give her maid as a substitute to bear children for her, so Sarah suggested Abraham take Hagar and let her bear his child. In his hurry, Abraham ran ahead of God and the consequences are still felt in the Middle East today. The Arab nations (descended from Ishmael, the son of the maid servant) and Israel (descended from Abraham's legitimate heir, Isaac) continue to be bitter enemies.

God not only has a divine will, He also has an eternal timetable. Just as the apostle Paul reminded Christians that in "the fullness of time" God sent His Son (Gal. 4:4) and "in due time Christ died for the ungodly" (Rom. 5:6), so God has a schedule for everything in our lives as well. We certainly don't want to lag behind God's agenda, but it's equally disastrous to run ahead of it.

As you seek God's will for your life, seek His timetable as well. Don't let your impatience carry you ahead of God. To do the right thing at the wrong time makes the right thing the wrong thing.

We need to keep in step with God's time as well as His will.

Reflections/Prayer Requests

_____

_____

_____

_____

_____

_____

DAY 17

Genesis 16:5-6

*Then Sarai said to Abram, "My wrong
be upon you! I gave my maid into your
embrace; and when she saw that she had
conceived, I became despised in her eyes.
The L*ORD *judge between you and me." So
Abram said to Sarai, "Indeed your maid is in
your hand; do to her as you please." And
when Sarai dealt harshly with her, she fled
from her presence.*

Who's in Charge?

A writer for the *Chicago Tribune* observed, "Americans crave leadership, but what is it?" According to an expert he quoted, a leader has "a moral compass, a set of core beliefs, a firmness that is not authoritarian, strong powers of persuasion in articulating a vision, and a self-effacing manner." Those qualities are not only scarce in the workplace, they're often lacking in the home as well.

In many respects, Abraham was a great leader, but apparently he wasn't strong enough to do what was right in his own household. At a time when Sarah needed a strong hand to guide her through a fit of jealousy, Abraham failed. He abdicated his role as the leader of his home and a grave injustice was committed as a result.

Our society needs strong leaders everywhere, but nowhere more than in the home. God established an order for the family that made it normative for the man to be the leader when present. The apostle Paul says, "For the husband is head of the wife . . . . Therefore, just as the church is subject to Christ, so let the wives be to their own husbands in everything" (Eph. 5:23-24; cf. 1 Cor. 11:3).

God's design for the family is not popular in today's culture, but it's still God's design. Men, take seriously your role as the head of the home. Know the core values God wants for your family and see that they are established. Wives, let your husband be the leader. Support him in his leadership and respect his authority. When we do what is right in the home, the nation will follow.

Leadership in the home is an issue of obedience, not equality.

Reflections/Prayer Requests

DAY 18

Genesis 17:1

*When Abram was ninety-nine years old, the
L<small>ORD</small> appeared to Abram and said to him, "I
am Almighty God; walk before Me and be
blameless."*

Complete in His Power

A farmer and his son were working
together in the field. The father told the
boy to throw all the large stones he could
find into a nearby ditch so they would not
interfere with plowing. After working a
long time, the son called out, "Dad, there's
one rock here I can't move even though
I've tried my hardest." "No, Son," replied
the father, "you haven't tried your hardest
until you've called for me to help you. I
can give you the strength you need." The
father came alongside the boy and added
his strength. Together, they moved the
stubborn rock with ease.

God also called upon Abraham to do
something that was impossible for him, if
tried under his own power. God commanded him to "walk before Me and be
blameless." The word *blameless* (Heb.
tamym) carries the sense of being complete, whole or mature. It implies a level of
integrity that is rarely found among men.
Such blamelessness would have been
impossible for Abraham, except for one

condition: the One who called him to such a level of maturity was the Almighty God.

Many people have tried to live the Christian life in their own power, and they all have failed. Some have come to believe that it's impossible to achieve such maturity in a sinful world. And, apart from the Almighty God, it is. But God said, "Behold, I am the LORD, the God of all flesh. Is there anything too hard for Me?" (Jer. 32:27). The apostle Paul said, "I can do *all things* through Christ who strengthens me" (Phil. 4:13, emphasis mine).

Cast yourself upon the mighty power of God. Only He is able to present you faultless before the throne. In His power your life can be complete and your walk can be blameless.

With God's power behind us, nothing can stand before us.

Reflections/Prayer Requests

_____

_____

_____

_____

_____

_____

_____

DAY 19

Genesis 17:3-6

Then Abram fell on his face, and God talked with him, saying: "As for Me, behold, My covenant is with you, and you shall be a father of many nations. No longer shall your name be called Abram, but your name shall be Abraham; for I have made you a father of many nations. I will make you exceedingly fruitful; and I will make nations of you, and kings shall come from you."

Get Off the Merry-go-round

An irate woman met her husband when he got off a merry-go-round and said, "Now, look at you. You spent your money, you got off right where you got on, and you haven't been anywhere!" Unfortunately, that's an accurate picture of life for many people today. But God has so much more to offer.

That was true with Abraham. The first 75 years he sought his fortune, first in Ur and later in Haran (Gen. 12:4). Then God called him to begin a journey that was both physical and spiritual. Abraham spent the next 24 years seeking to follow his God. However, he also spent a good deal of time living by his own wits instead of trusting the Lord. Finally, shortly before reaching the century mark, he learned the secret. He "fell on his face." Abraham totally surrendered to God, and it was then that God gave His most spectacular promises. From Abram (Father of Height), God changed his name to Abraham (Father of a Multitude). From an obscure desert sheik, he became the forerunner of kings and nations.

For those willing to submit to Him, God has an abundant life in store. In fact, the apostle Paul reminds us, "Eye has not seen, nor ear heard, nor have entered into the heart of man the things which God has prepared for those who love Him" (1 Cor. 2:9).

If life seems a bit like a merry-go-round to you, maybe it's time to discover God's abundant life. Surrender yourself completely to Him and find a life more fulfilling than you can imagine.

The abundant life comes not by accumulating but by letting go.

Reflections/Prayer Requests

DAY 20

Genesis 17:17

Then Abraham fell on his face and laughed, and said in his heart, "Shall a child be born to a man who is one hundred years old? And shall Sarah, who is ninety years old, bear a child?"

A Rest for Your Faith

When John Paton was translating the Bible for a South Pacific island tribe, he discovered that they had no word for trust or faith. One day a native who had been running hard came into the missionary's house, flopped down in a large chair and said, "It's good to rest my whole weight on this chair." "That's it!" exclaimed Paton. "I'll translate faith as 'resting one's whole weight on God.'"

Abraham was a man of faith—but sometimes that faith was in the wrong place. When God told him he would have a son, he looked at himself and said, "Shall a child be born to a man who is one hundred years old?" Obviously, from a human perspective that was a ridiculous notion. Instead of resting his faith wholly upon God, Abraham was trying to carry part of the burden himself.

Faith always falters when we trust in our own capabilities. If something was doable by human standards, faith would not be necessary. The essence of faith requires that it is something that can be accomplished only if God undertakes it for us. The ultimate example of this, of course, is our own salvation. When He was asked, "Who then can be saved?" Jesus responded, "The things which are impossible with men are possible with God" (Luke 18:27). The apostle Paul declares in Philippians 4:13, "I can do all things," but then he goes on to clarify, "through Christ who strengthens me." It is not we who can do all things, but Christ.

Where is your faith resting? Are you depending upon your own resources, or are you resting your whole weight upon God? Whether it's for your ultimate salvation or some daily responsibility, have faith in God. Only He can do the impossible.

What the world calls ridiculous, God calls faith.

Reflections/Prayer Requests

_____

_____

_____

_____

_____

_____

DAY 21

Genesis 17:10

"This is My covenant which you shall keep, between Me and you and your descendants after you: Every male child among you shall be circumcised."

Genesis 17:22-23

Then He finished talking with him, and God went up from Abraham. So Abraham took Ishmael his son, all who were born in his house and all who were bought with his money, every male among the men of Abraham's house, and circumcised the flesh of their foreskins that very same day, as God had said to him.

Instant Obedience

Supermarkets are filled with all kinds of instant products—instant pudding, instant coffee, instant soup, instant potatoes and so much more. We seem to want everything instantly these days. Unfortunately, no supermarket stocks instant obedience.

Throughout his years of walking with the Lord, Abraham learned that the best type of obedience was instant obedience. When God declared circumcision to be the sign of His covenant with Abraham and his descendants, this desert potentate lost no time in seeing that every male in his household was circumcised. Nor did he

44

exclude himself. It was not a matter of "I direct; you perform." At the age of 99, Abraham subjected himself to the same temporary discomfort as everyone else. Doing God's will knows no rank or privileges.

This same instant obedience should be a part of our walk today. To become a Christian is relatively simple; to live like one is another matter. We become a Christian by repentant faith; we live as a Christian only as we obey Christ's commands. The extent of that commitment is measured by the speed with which we obey. The Holy Spirit says through the writer of Hebrews, "*Today*, if you will hear His voice, do not harden your hearts as in the rebellion, in the day of trial in the wilderness" (Heb. 3:7-8, emphasis mine).

If the Lord has been speaking to you about a matter of obedience, stop delaying. The blessing you receive by doing God's will is directly proportional to the speed with which you begin to do it.

Salvation is through faith; maturity is through obedience.

Reflections/Prayer Requests

DAY 22

Genesis 18:2-3

So he lifted his eyes and looked, and behold, three men were standing by him; and when he saw them, he ran from the tent door to meet them, and bowed himself to the ground, and said, "My Lord, if I have now found favor in Your sight, do not pass on by Your servant."

Angels Unaware

"Old Bill" was hired to sweep streets in a small town. During the hot days of July and August, Mrs. Brown on the corner got into the habit of taking him a glass of lemonade and a slice of cake. He thanked her shyly and that was all. But one evening there came a knock at the back door of her home. Bill was there with a sack of apples in one hand and a handful of roasting ears in the other. He said, "I brought you these, Ma'am, for your kindness." "Oh, you shouldn't have," exclaimed Mrs. Brown. "It was nothing." "Well, no," the street sweeper agreed, "maybe it wasn't much, but it was more than anyone else did."

Abraham was equally aware of the needs of those around him. When three strangers appeared in front of his tent, he was more than eager to extend hospitality to them. He could have thought, *Surely someone who is less busy than I am will have compassion on them.* But he didn't.

Instead, he ran to meet them and begged for an opportunity to show hospitality to these travelers.

The Bible says that hospitality is to characterize the Christian life. In fact, it's so important that it's listed as one of the qualifications for anyone desiring a position of leadership in the church (1 Tim. 3:2, Titus 1:8). The writer of Hebrews said, "Do not forget to entertain strangers, for by so doing some have unwittingly entertained angels" (Heb. 13:2).

Do yourself a favor: when you have opportunity to open your home to a troubled teenager or to host a foreign student while the dorms are closed, do it! You never know when you might come across an angel.

Some may have the gift of hospitality, but we all have the responsibility.

Reflections/Prayer Requests

_____

_____

_____

_____

_____

_____

_____

DAY 23

Genesis 18:17-19

*And the L*ORD *said, "Shall I hide from Abraham what I am doing, since Abraham shall
surely become a great and mighty nation,
and all the nations of the earth shall be
blessed in him? For I have known him,
in order that he may command his children
and his household after him, that they keep
the way of the L*ORD*, to do righteousness
and justice, that the L*ORD *may bring to Abraham what He has spoken to him."*

Intimate Fellowship

It's a shame, but some people think
they can get to know God by taking drugs.
One person wrote to a religious columnist
that drugs should be legalized because he
felt close to God when he smoked pot. But
drugs are dangerous to a person's physical and mental health, and they are not a
pipeline to God. What a person experi-
ences while under the influence of drugs
does not originate with God.

Abraham had an intimate relationship
with God and he used no mood-altering
stimulants to get it. God made a conscious
choice not to hide anything from Abraham. There were no secrets between
them. Furthermore, it was a relationship
based on mutual trust. God said, "For I
have known him." God knew everything

about Abraham—past, present and future—and loved him anyway.

We can enjoy this same intimacy. God revealed everything we need to know about Him in the Bible. He took the initiative to clear away the stumbling blocks of sin by offering His Son as our Savior. There is nothing that He desires more than to have an intimate relationship with us.

Now it's time for you to do your part. Be as open with God as He is with you. Set aside time to get to know Him better. Seek Him daily in the Scriptures. Speak with Him often through prayer. Look for His guidance in your life. The result will be an intimacy that no drug can ever produce.

An intimate relationship with God is based on character, not chemicals.

Reflections/Prayer Requests

_____

_____

_____

_____

_____

_____

_____

_____

_____

DAY 24

Genesis 21:1-3

And the LORD visited Sarah as He had said, and the LORD did for Sarah as He had spoken. For Sarah conceived and bore Abraham a son in his old age, at the set time of which God had spoken to him. And Abraham called the name of his son who was born to him—whom Sarah bore to him—Isaac.

Joy to the World

Someone asked Joseph Haydn, the famous composer, why his music was so cheerful. He replied, "I cannot make it otherwise. When I think upon God, my heart is so full of joy that the notes dance and leap from my pen!"

This must have been the way that Abraham and Sarah felt. After Abraham waited 100 years and Sarah reached the matronly age of 90, God gave them a son. Joy surely leapt and danced in their hearts. In fact, they named their son Isaac, which means "laughter." Unlike the laughter of unbelief they had engaged in earlier (Gen. 17:17, 18:12), this laughter percolated through a holy wonder at the miracle in their life. It was a laughter of such unalloyed joy that all who heard it laughed with them (21:6).

The joy that began with the birth of Isaac, however, reached its crescendo in the birth of Jesus. When the angels

50

announced their heavenly message, they proclaimed, "Do not be afraid, for behold, I bring you good tidings of *great joy* which will be to all people" (Luke 2:10, emphasis mine). Jesus said, "These things I have spoken to you, that My joy may remain in you, and that your joy may be full" (John 15:11).

When was the last time you laughed for the sheer joy of your salvation? People are not attracted to somber doctrines. There is no persuasive power in a gloomy and morbid religion. Let the world see your joy and you won't be able to keep them away.

To be filled with God is to be filled with joy.

Reflections/Prayer Requests

_____

_____

_____

_____

_____

_____

_____

_____

_____

_____

_____

DAY 25

Genesis 21:9-11

And Sarah saw the son of Hagar the Egyptian, whom she had borne to Abraham, scoffing. Therefore she said to Abraham, "Cast out this bondwoman and her son; for the son of this bondwoman shall not be heir with my son, namely with Isaac." And the matter was very displeasing in Abraham's sight because of his son.

Truth or Consequences

Solomon Garcia of Huntington, New York, was crushed to death by a 600-pound safe he apparently was trying to steal. Suffolk County police lieutenant John Gierasch said that the young man was trying to move the iron safe down some stairs of a real estate and insurance company office when it slipped. A maintenance man found the body under the safe at the base of a first-floor staircase.

When we violate God's truth, His Word, consequences always result. Sometimes those consequences are tragic. Abraham discovered this. In his hurry to make God's promise of a son come true, he agreed to take Sarah's servant, Hagar, as a substitute wife. The child born from that union, however, was not God's intended heir. When Isaac, the son of promise, was born, a rivalry developed that eventually caused Sarah to demand Hagar and her son leave the house. Abraham's disobedience brought serious consequences, not only to himself but to everyone he loved. Only God's intervention prevented a tragedy (Gen. 21:16-19).

When we fail to obey God's truth, we can expect consequences. This is not because God is out to get even. Instead, it's because God's truth protects us from situations that will harm us. When we trample down those protective fences God has set up in His Word, we end up experiencing the evil from which those fences were created to save us.

Take God at His word. The Scriptures can keep you from harm. Refuse to violate God's truth either by running ahead or lagging behind His will for your life. God's truth will keep you from the consequences.

Accept the Truth and avoid the consequences.

Reflections/Prayer Requests

_____

_____

_____

_____

_____

_____

_____

DAY 26

Now it came to pass after these things that God tested Abraham, and said to him, "Abraham!" And he said, "Here I am." And He said, "Take now your son, your only son Isaac, whom you love, and go to the land of Moriah, and offer him there as a burnt offering on one of the mountains of which I shall tell you."

The Ultimate Sacrifice

C. S. Lewis said, "To love at all is to be vulnerable. Love anything, and your heart will certainly be wrung and possibly be broken."

Abraham must have felt that way. He had waited 25 years to receive the blessing that God had promised him on the day he packed up his family and possessions and left Haran. He had waited 100 years to receive a very special son. How his heart must have ached when God commanded him to take his only son, his precious Isaac, and sacrifice him as a burnt offering on Mount Moriah. Even though he responded in faith, we can't imagine the hurt. It was the ultimate sacrifice.

But Abraham is not the only one who was ever asked to make an ultimate sacrifice. God, too, gave His only begotten Son. The apostle Paul reminds us that God "did not spare His own Son, but delivered Him up for us all" (Rom. 8:32). And Peter draws our attention to the fact that "you were not redeemed with corruptible things, like silver or gold, from your aimless conduct received by tradition from your fathers, but with the precious blood of Christ, as of a lamb without blemish and without spot" (1 Pet. 1:18-19). God knows the pain of an ultimate sacrifice.

Has God asked you to make a sacrifice? Perhaps it's been the loss of a child, a cancer diagnosis, a bankruptcy. Do you feel that your life is in ashes, hopeless and irrecoverable? Lift your eyes to the Lord. Ask Him to meet you at the point of your need. God understands. He will comfort you.

The greater the pain, the greater the compassion.

Reflections/Prayer Requests

_____

_____

_____

_____

_____

_____

_____

_____

DAY 27

Genesis 22:7-8

But Isaac spoke to Abraham his father and said, "My father!" And he said, "Here I am, my son." Then he said, "Look, the fire and the wood, but where is the lamb for a burnt offering?" And Abraham said, "My son, God will provide for Himself the lamb for a burnt offering." And the two of them went together.

Divine Provision

A young girl was taking a long journey, and in the course of her travels her train had to cross a number of rivers. Each time the train approached water, her doubts were awakened. She didn't understand how such raging torrents could safely be crossed. As they drew near the river, however, a bridge invariably appeared and provided the way over. Finally the little girl leaned back with a sigh of relief and said with confidence, "Somebody has put bridges for us all the way!"

Abraham showed the same confidence as he faced the possibility of sacrificing his only son. Never had his faith been more severely tested. Yet he could confidently reply to Isaac, "God will supply the lamb." Abraham didn't know *how* God was going to do it, but he believed without reservation that God would.

That same confidence can be yours and mine. We often don't know how God will provide. He may supply in a way that we would not have chosen. That is not for us to say. Our assurance is that God will meet our needs, however He chooses. The apostle Paul reminds us, "And my God shall supply all your need according to His riches in glory by Christ Jesus" (Phil. 4:19).

God may meet your need for healing by miraculously restoring your body. Or, He may choose to give you the strength to endure an illness with courage. God may relieve your financial situation through a generous gift. Then again, He may provide just enough to get you through each month. *How* He meets your need is evidence of His sovereignty. *That* He meets your need is evidence of His grace. It's not necessary that we know how, as long as we know Him.

Our need is simply an opportunity for God's provision.

Reflections/Prayer Requests

_____

_____

_____

_____

_____

_____

_____

DAY 28

Genesis 22:9-10

*Then they came to the place of which God
had told him. And Abraham built an altar
there and placed the wood in order; and he
bound Isaac his son and laid him on the altar,
upon the wood. And Abraham stretched out
his hand and took the knife to slay his son.*

Making Sense

Pablo Picasso was the most famous
painter of the 20th century. His paintings
often broke with the traditional notion of
beauty and harmony. When questioned
about his unusual artistic style, the distin-
guished painter replied, "The world today
doesn't make sense, so why should I paint
pictures that do?" Many people would
probably agree with his observation.
Often the world doesn't seem to make
sense.

Surely this thought must have passed
through Abraham's mind when God commanded him to sacrifice his son. After all,
Abraham had waited 100 years for the
birth of this child. But there was more
involved here than paternal love. God had
made significant promises with world-
wide implications based on Abraham's
descendants. It simply didn't make sense
for Abraham now to take this essential
link to the future welfare of the world and
offer him as a sacrifice.

Fortunately, if this thought did pass through Abraham's mind, it didn't stay. He bound his son on the altar and lifted the sacrificial knife. He had learned from his past mistakes never to question God and never to delay obeying Him. With a faith that took captive his feelings, he prepared to do exactly as God commanded.

The lesson of Abraham is clear. It is not necessary to understand; it is only necessary to obey. The prophet Samuel reminds us, "To obey is better than sacrifice, and to heed than the fat of rams" (1 Sam. 15:22). Jesus said, "If you love Me, keep My commandments" (John 14:15).

If God is calling you to take a step of faith that defies earthly wisdom, put obedience first and let logic catch up.

If you can't understand the why, trust the Who.

Reflections/Prayer Requests

_____

_____

_____

_____

_____

_____

_____

_____

DAY 29

Genesis 22:18

*In your seed all the nations of the earth
shall be blessed, because you have obeyed
My voice.*

Make My Life a Blessing

The creed for a lot of parents these days is, "Get even. Live long enough to be a problem to your kids." That's humorous, and in some circumstances, understandable, but it's not very good advice. Abraham's life illustrates a different approach: he lived long enough to be a blessing.

Think what we might have missed had Abraham died at an earlier age. During his first 75 years, he lived as a dutiful son to his father, Terah, and a faithful husband to his wife, Sarah. He was a blessing to these two, but there were many others ahead. Through years of tests and trials God purified his life and taught him obedience. Then finally, at age 99, he stood ready to be a blessing to the whole world. Through his son, born when Abraham was 100, came the Messiah, who would bring hope and salvation to "all the nations of the earth."

Christians should view each year God gives us as an opportunity to be an even greater blessing to those around us. The older we grow, the more blessed our presence should be. We must be careful that the years don't simply increase our litany of complaints or add to our list of ailments. Let's seal our lips against giving unwanted advice; let's be available but not meddlesome. Instead of seeking how we can be blessed, let's seek to be a blessing instead.

Whose life might you bless today? Is there someone you can encourage with a note or phone call? Is there an act of kindness you might do for a neighbor? Accumulate more for yourself than just the years you live; collect the opportunities to be a blessing to others.

Live life to be a blessing, not a bystander.

Reflections/Prayer Requests

_____

_____

_____

_____

_____

_____

_____

_____

_____

_____

DAY 30

Genesis 23:12-13

Then Abraham bowed himself down before the people of the land; and he spoke to Ephron in the hearing of the people of the land, saying, "If you will give it, please hear me. I will give you money for the field; take it from me and I will bury my dead there."

Guarding the Golden Years

Before and after the Civil War, the Reverend Henry Ward Beecher was the most famous preacher in America. He drew crowds of thousands to his church in Brooklyn each week. He reportedly earned the princely sum of $40,000 per year. Delighting in his treasures, Beecher enjoyed carrying with him uncut gems and openly endorsed commercial products ranging from soap to watches. Then in 1874, Beecher's friend and protégé, Theodore Tilton, accused the preacher of seducing his wife. His trial was such an attraction that admission tickets were sold to the public. The jury failed to reach a verdict, but Beecher's influence and popularity continued undiminished for another 13 years until his death.

What a contrast this is with the closing days of Abraham's life. While he had faltered in his earlier years, failing to fully trust the Lord, he spent his latter days as a shining example of a man who had total faith in God. Even in the midst of his grief, as he prepared to bury his beloved Sarah, he maintained his integrity. Confronted with the exorbitant request for 400 shekels of silver for a plot of ground, he courteously conceded. Refusing to lower himself to the level of a Bedouin huckster, he demonstrated the graciousness of a man who had learned to put his life in God's hands.

Great Christians are not great because of what they say; they're great because of what they do. And what they do during their darkest days is the best indicator of their integrity.

The latter years of every Christian should be our best. A good start is a wonderful thing, but a good finish is even better.

Make sure your golden years are more than gold-plated.

Reflections/Prayer Requests

_____

_____

_____

_____

_____

_____

_____

DAY 31

Genesis 25:8, 11

*Then Abraham breathed his last and died
in a good old age, an old man and full
of years, and was gathered to his people.
And it came to pass, after the death of
Abraham, that God blessed his son Isaac.
And Isaac dwelt at Beer Lahai Roi.*

Pass It On

A man's character often lives on long
after he is gone. Take Jonathan Edwards,
for example. He loved the Lord and taught
his children to do the same. According to
one estimate, he has had 929 descendants. Of these, 430 were ministers; 86
were university professors; 13 became
university presidents; 75 authored good
books; and 7 were elected to the United
States Congress. One was vice president
of his nation. Edwards left a spiritual heritage that became a blessing not only for
his descendants, but for all of society.

Abraham did the same. At the age of
175 he was "gathered to his people." But
that wasn't the end. Abraham passed on
to his son a spiritual heritage that brought
God's blessing upon Isaac and, down
through the centuries, to all of us through
Jesus Christ, a distant descendant of this
godly patriarch. Abraham didn't merely
"pass on"; he made it possible for God to

pass on His blessings through his descendants.

We all need to live with future generations in mind. It's not enough to live a godly life to gain God's blessings for yourself; consider what influence your life will have on your grandchildren, your great-grandchildren and the rest of your family tree. The character you choose to develop will leave its mark on the lives of generations you'll never live to see.

Don't be content to leave an inheritance of material possessions. Instead, strive to be a channel for God's blessings to reach generations still unborn. The greatest inheritance your posterity can receive from you is the heritage of God's blessing.

Live so your descendants will rise up and call you blessed.

Reflections/Prayer Requests

_____

_____

_____

_____

_____

_____

_____